THE LEAR  P9-CMY-212

Weston Intermediate School

THE
GOLDEN
RETRIEVER

by Charlotte Wilcox

THE LEARNING RESOURCE CENTER
Weston Intermediate School

C. 1

CAPSTONE
HIGH-INTEREST
BOOKS

an imprint of Capstone Press
Mankato, Minnesota

Capstone Books are published by Capstone Press
151 Good Counsel Drive, P.O. Box 669, Mankato, Minnesota 56002
http://www.capstone-press.com

Copyright © 1996 Capstone Press. All rights reserved.
No part of this book may be reproduced without written permission from the
publisher. The publisher takes no responsibility for the use of any of the
materials or methods described in this book, nor for the products thereof.
Printed in the United States of America.

Library of Congress Cataloging-in-Publication Data
Wilcox, Charlotte.
      The Golden retriever/by Charlotte Wilcox
      p. cm.--(Learning about dogs)
      Includes bibliographical references (p. 46) and index.
      Summary: An introduction to this friendly dog, which includes its
      history, development, uses, and care.
      ISBN 1-56065-397-3
      1. Golden retrievers--Juvenile literature. [1. Golden Retrievers.] I. Title.
      II. Series: Wilcox, Charlotte. Learning about dogs.
SF429.G63W54 1996
636.7'52--dc20

                                                 96-26571
                                                   CIP
                                                    AC

Photo Credits
Archive Photos, 18, 30
Bill Smith, 12
FPG, 8, 10, 16, 36
Reynolds Photography, 4, 6, 14, 28, 34, 38-39
Sue Reynolds, 20
Unicorn, cover, Chris Boylan, 22, 24; David Cummings, 32; John Ebeling, 26;
Paul Murphy, 40

2 3 4 5 6 05 04 03 02 01

Table of Contents

Words in **boldface** type in the text are defined in the Glossary in the back of this book.

Quick Facts about the Golden Retriever

Description

Height: Males stand 23 to 24 inches (58 to 61 centimeters) and females stand 20 to 22-1/2 inches (51 to 57 centimeters) from the ground to the top of the shoulders.

Weight: Males weigh 65 to 75 pounds (29 to 34 kilograms) and females weigh 55 to 65 pounds (25 to 29 kilograms).

Physical features:	Goldens are active dogs with strong muscles, straight **muzzles**, medium-sized ears that fold close to the head, and thick coats and tails.
Color:	Goldens are shades of gold from light blond to reddish.

Development

Place of origin:	Goldens originated in England and Scotland.
History of breed:	Goldens descended from a yellow puppy born into a litter of black retrievers. They were later crossed with **spaniel**, Irish **setter**, and bloodhound breeds.
Numbers:	Almost 65,000 goldens are **registered** in the United States every year, and about 8,500 in Canada. Many more are born that are not registered.

Uses

Golden retrievers were developed for hunting. They also make good **guide dogs**, police dogs, search-and-rescue dogs, and family pets.

Chapter 1
The Perfect Dog

The golden retriever is one of the most popular dogs in North America. Goldens love people. They enjoy running and playing. They are sweet and gentle.

The golden retriever got its name from its color and its actions. Goldens are known for their beautiful gold coats that are mostly waterproof. They were bred to retrieve **game** birds. Retrieve means to go get something and carry it back. Goldens are good retrievers on land, but they are excellent in the water.

The Golden retriever is one of the friendliest dog breeds.

Goldens are also very easy to train. They can be trained as police dogs, seeing-eye dogs, **signal dogs**, and **service dogs**.

Golden retrievers are part of a larger family of retriever dogs. Retrievers were bred to find and bring back dead and wounded birds to hunters. Many goldens still work in this way. Others are faithful companions to people and families.

Goldens are popular as hunting dogs and as family pets. Some people think the golden retriever is the perfect dog.

Golden retrievers are part of a large family of retriever dogs, which includes many other breeds.

Chapter 2

Beginnings of the Breed

People and dogs have hunted together for thousands of years. A dog's sharp nose and ears can find game better than a person can. A human with a weapon can kill game that a dog cannot. Together they make an unbeatable team.

The First Retrievers

Early hunters used spears or bows. A spear hunter had to get close enough to the game to spear it. A bow hunter could be a little farther away. Sometimes an animal hit by an arrow ran away or fell into water or tall grass. Bow

Golden retrievers are sometimes called gun dogs.

Golden retrievers are a popular hunting dog.

hunters taught dogs to find and retrieve the game.

When Europeans began using guns, hunters could kill game from much farther away. It became even harder to find shot game. Retriever dogs became more important to their human hunting partners. People bred the best dogs they could find for the qualities they needed. They called them **gun dogs**.

Hunters in England and Scotland developed gun dogs that were good at retrieving birds. They needed dogs that were strong enough to carry large birds in their mouths. They had to be small enough to crawl through bushes without getting caught in the branches. They had to be good swimmers. They needed waterproof coats for retrieving in icy-cold water. They needed to be gentle enough to bring back a bird without damaging the meat.

Wealthy hunters in England and Scotland had kennels where they bred the best dogs. Many of today's popular hunting dogs were developed in England, Ireland, and Scotland during the 1800s. These include springer spaniels, English and Irish setters, and curly-coated and flat-coated retrievers.

Early Flat-Coats

Flat-coated retrievers were top bird dogs. They were good swimmers for retrieving ducks

The golden retriever breed started with one yellow puppy.

and geese. They also did well at retrieving such land birds as pheasants and partridge. Their thick, waterproof coats were usually black or liver-colored. Liver is a reddish-brown color.

Owners of flat-coated retrievers were careful to breed only dogs that had these qualities. Sometimes a yellow puppy would be born in a litter of black or liver-colored retrievers. Puppies with the wrong color or the wrong type of coat were often killed.

The Yellow Puppy

One day in the mid-1860s, on an English estate, a black retriever had a litter of puppies. They were all black except one. The odd puppy had a brilliant golden coat. The owner gave the puppy away.

The little yellow puppy ended up living in a clothing shop. Sir Dudley Majoriebanks, an Englishman, found him there. Sir Dudley, also called Lord Tweedmouth, was working to breed the perfect gun dog. This unwanted yellow puppy was exactly what he was looking for. He named the puppy Nous. The name is a British word that rhymes with loose and means alert or sensible.

Lord Tweedmouth took Nous to his farm in Scotland and searched for a mate for the dog. In 1868, he chose a liver-colored spaniel named Belle. Two months later, Belle had four gold-colored puppies. They were named Crocus, Primrose, Cowslip, and Ada. They are the ancestors of the golden retriever breed.

Chapter 3

Development of the Breed

With Nous and Belle's four puppies, Lord Tweedmouth got just what he wanted. The puppies were strong, of medium size, and good swimmers with golden, waterproof coats. They were smart and had a lot of energy. And they loved people.

The puppies also had soft mouths to gently carry game. This is one of the traits of golden retrievers. Their mouths are not soft like a pillow. They are soft like a hug.

The Four Puppies Grow Up

Over the next few years, Lord Tweedmouth carefully chose mates for his four golden puppies and their puppies. He used spaniels and other retrievers to increase the breed's strength. An Irish setter improved their color. A bloodhound

Golden retrievers have mouths that are soft like a hug. This is good for retrieving game without harming it.

The golden retriever has a waterproof coat for retrieving from lakes and rivers.

improved their sense of smell. Other breeders followed Lord Tweedmouth's lead. They bred their dogs for the same combination of talent, looks, and personality.

No one knows for sure how many golden puppies Crocus, Cowslip, Primrose, and Ada had during their lives, but there were many. Cowslip had puppies until she was more than 20 years old. Most of the golden retrievers living today can trace their ancestors back to these four English puppies.

During the late 1800s, bird hunting was a popular sport. At this time, golden retrievers found their way to fame. They could find a wounded bird in the thickest bushes, tallest grass, or deepest water. They would bring it back every time. They never seemed to get bored during a long day of hunting.

Part of the Family

Hunters soon began to see that the golden retriever was not only a good hunting partner, but also a wonderful friend. The same golden that loved to retrieve also loved to play with the hunter's children at home.

Goldens became part of the family. They tagged along with children walking to school. They followed farmers through the fields. They listened to bedtime stories with the family. They seemed to enjoy all these activities as much as hunting. They just wanted to be with the people they loved.

Chapter 4

The Golden Retriever Today

In 1881, one of Lord Tweedmouth's relatives brought the first golden retriever to Canada. In 1894, the first golden came into the United States. By 1900, many goldens lived in American and Canadian homes as gun dogs and pets.

Registering Dogs

Kennel clubs keep track of the **pedigrees** of dogs. The American Kennel Club, the

The golden retriever is one of the most popular breeds in the United States and Canada.

For a puppy to be registered, both its parents must already be registered.

Canadian Kennel Club, and the Kennel Club of England have pedigrees of dogs going back to the 1800s. For a puppy to be registered as a certain breed, both of the puppy's parents must already be registered as that breed. This rule helps keep each breed's special qualities strong.

Golden retrievers were first registered with the Kennel Club of England in 1903. Before that, Lord Tweedmouth and other breeders kept their own records. Because of them, we know the pedigrees of many golden retrievers all the way back to Nous and Belle.

In North America, some goldens were registered in the early 1900s as flat-coated retrievers. In 1925, the American Kennel Club recognized the golden retriever as a separate breed. Two years later, the Canadian Kennel Club recognized them. The golden retriever remains one of the most popular breeds in both countries.

Golden Retriever Clubs

In 1911, a woman in England organized the first golden retriever club. Today, there are golden retriever clubs in many countries. The Golden Retriever Club of America began in 1938. It is one of the largest dog clubs in the United States. The Golden Retriever Club of Canada began in 1958. These national clubs oversee many local golden retriever clubs.

What a Golden Retriever Looks Like

Like all retrievers, goldens are medium-sized dogs with strong bones and muscles. Males are 23 to 24 inches (58 to 61 centimeters) tall and weigh 65 to 75 pounds (29 to 34 kilograms). Females are a little smaller. They are 20 to 22-1/2 inches (51 to 57 centimeters) tall and weigh 55 to 65 pounds (25 to 29 kilograms).

The first thing most people notice about the golden retriever is its rich gold coat. The shade can vary from pale yellow to a deep reddish gold. They should have no white or dark markings. Golden retrievers have brown eyes and a black nose. Their medium-sized ears fold close to their heads.

Another thing people notice is that goldens always seem to look happy. Their mouths turn up at the corners, so they look like they are smiling. And their tails always seem to be wagging.

Goldens always seem to look happy because their mouths turn up at the corners.

Chapter 5

The Golden Retriever in Action

Golden retrievers are among the most popular pets in North America. Though they love the outdoors, many do well inside if they get enough exercise and attention. They want to feel like part of a family.

Most goldens love children. They seem to know that children want to play, and they love to play along. They do not seem to mind the tumbling and tugging that bother some dogs.

Older people enjoy the loyal friendship of golden retrievers, too. Goldens never seem to get bored as long as they can be with people. They do not make the best watchdogs because they are too friendly. But most do a good job of barking to let their owner know when someone is at the door.

Most goldens love to be outside and to play.

Golden retrievers often participate in field trials.

Hunting Dogs Forever

Many goldens head for the open fields on weekends with their owners. The golden retriever's patience, intelligence, and obedience make hunting enjoyable for both hunter and dog.

For more than a century, gun-dog owners have shown off their dogs in events called field trials. These events are held to judge hunting dogs on their ability to retrieve. Field trials are held in wildlife, wetland, or farming areas with plenty of open space. Often there are ponds or streams.

The dog and its **handler** watch from some distance away. A helper called a gunner releases a duck or pheasant. The bird flies up. The gunner shoots it, and it falls into the grass or water. Then the dog must retrieve it.

If the dog saw where the bird fell, he should go directly to it and bring it back to the handler. If the dog did not see where the bird fell, the handler uses a whistle and hand signals to guide the dog to the dead bird. The dog earns points for how quickly it finds and retrieves the bird.

Police Dogs

Golden retrievers make good partners for police officers who need to search for things. With their supersensitive noses, they can sniff out hidden bombs or illegal drugs. Their obedient

Goldens can be trained to help a person with a disability.

nature is helpful when the dog and the officer are in dangerous situations.

One famous search dog was a golden retriever named Trep. His owner was a police officer whose job was to find illegal drugs. Trep sniffed out millions of dollars' worth of illegal drugs. He helped his owner arrest at least 100 drug dealers.

One day, the officer took Trep to a school. He wanted to show off Trep's talents to the students.

Before Trep arrived, another officer hid 10 packages of drugs around the school. Trep came into the school and began to sniff his way down the halls. One by one, Trep led the officers to the 10 packages of drugs. But, he did not stop there. He also led them to another package of illegal drugs. Someone at the school was busted that day.

Helping the Disabled

Dogs that help disabled persons are among the most intelligent and highly trained dogs in the world. Guide dogs for the blind must be obedient and able to lead. Golden retrievers are among the most popular guide dogs. Their calm, friendly attitude makes them good at leading their blind owners through crowds and traffic.

Some golden retrievers are signal dogs for people who cannot hear. They alert their owners to things like an alarm clock, telephone, or fire alarm ringing, or a baby crying. Other goldens work as service dogs for people in wheelchairs. They turn lights on and off, open doors, retrieve things, and even pull the wheelchair.

Chapter 6

A Golden Retriever of Your Own

Thousands of families own a golden retriever. Owning a dog is an important responsibility. Families must make sure they can provide what the golden retriever needs to be safe, healthy, and happy.

Finding a Golden Retriever

The best place to buy a purebred golden retriever is from a breeder. You can contact the golden retriever club in your area to find a good one. If you want a hunting dog, you need to find one whose parents are good hunting dogs.

Another good place to find a golden retriever is at a rescue shelter. This is a home for orphaned animals. Maybe they were abandoned or lost. Maybe their former owners

Goldens like to chew on chew toys. But never give it a bone that could get stuck in its throat.

A golden retriever needs a place to get some exercise.

could not keep them. Dogs in shelters can make good pets, but they may not be purebred goldens.

Most cities have an animal shelter listed in the telephone book. Some large cities have shelters just for golden retrievers. Workers at rescue shelters try to find good homes for them. They make sure the dogs are healthy and safe for families. Many of the dogs are full grown and already have some training.

Keeping a Golden

A golden retriever needs plenty of exercise and a lot of love and attention. Pet goldens do best living with people. The dog needs a small corner that is all its own. The area should have a food dish, water dish, and a dog bed or cage with a blanket.

A retriever also needs to spend time outside. If you have a yard, you will need a dog-proof fence, a place where the dog can get out of the sun and wind, and some toys. If you do not have a yard, you should take your dog walking for at least an hour every day.

Hunting goldens do better living outside. Hunting dogs that live indoors sometimes lose their hunting talents.

Even the most loving, gentle golden retriever can benefit from obedience training. If your new dog is not already trained, the training should start the first day you bring it home. If you have never trained a dog before, you will need help from someone who has. Or you can learn from books about training dogs.

Golden retrievers do not need much grooming.

To make sure you can find your dog if it gets lost, have your name and telephone number engraved on the collar. You could also have a **veterinarian** implant a microchip under its skin. A microchip is a computer chip about the size of a grain of rice. When scanned, it will tell the owner's name, address, and telephone number.

A Retriever's Food

The best diet for a dog is good-quality packaged dog food. You may give your dog a few table scraps once in a while as a treat, but never give bones that the dog could chew up and swallow. They could get caught in its throat or damage the inside of its body.

The amount of food a dog eats depends on its size, age, and how much exercise it gets. A full-grown golden retriever may eat about a pound (half a kilogram) of dry dog food, or a pound and a half (a little more than half a kilogram) of semimoist dog food, or two large cans of canned food every day. Many owners divide the food into two meals, but one meal a day is fine, too.

Dogs need plenty of water. If you cannot have fresh water out all the time, make sure your dog drinks at least three times a day.

Grooming

Golden retrievers do not need much grooming. Brushing your dog every few days will usually keep its hair clean and free of

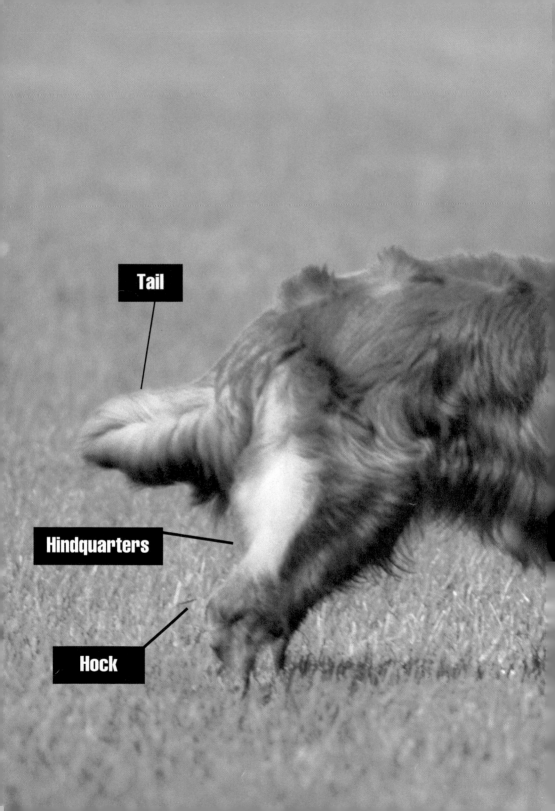

Tail

Hindquarters

Hock

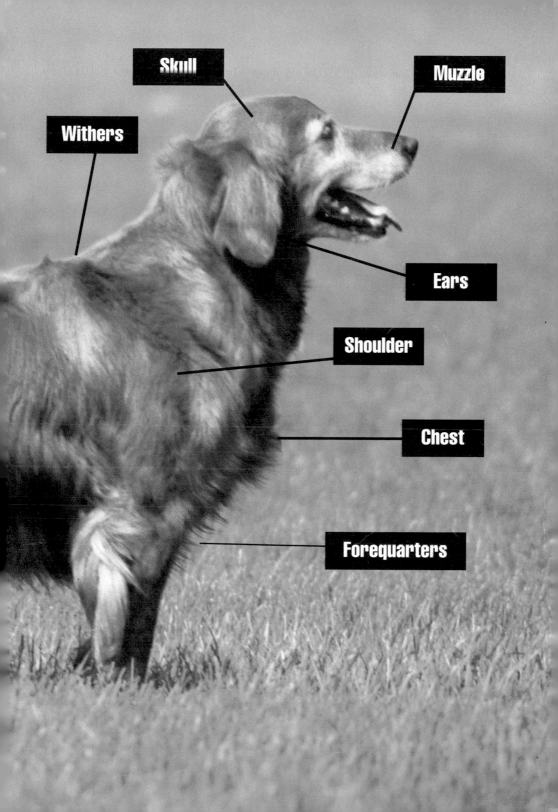

Skull

Muzzle

Withers

Ears

Shoulder

Chest

Forequarters

Goldens should visit the vet for regular checkups.

tangles. Do not give your golden a bath too often because it could cause shedding. Use only shampoo made just for dogs.

Give your dog a rawhide bone to chew to help keep its teeth healthy. Also, brush its teeth with a dog toothbrush and toothpaste regularly. Never use human toothpaste on a dog. Trim your dog's nails only if they get too long. Take the dog to a veterinarian or professional groomer the first time to see how to do it.

A Healthy Golden Retriever

Dogs need shots every year to protect them from **rabies**, **distemper**, and other diseases. They can kill a dog. Some can spread to humans. Dogs also need pills to protect them from **heartworms**. These enter the dog's heart and slowly destroy it. A checkup is needed every year for all types of worms.

During warm weather, check for ticks. Some ticks carry **Lyme disease**, a serious illness that can cripple a dog or human. Humans cannot catch Lyme disease from dogs, but they can get it from the same tick that bit the dog. Put rubbing alcohol on the tick and pull it out with tweezers. Drown it in the alcohol or bleach. Check often for fleas, lice, and mites. These are tiny insects that make the dog scratch itself. Special sprays and shampoos usually get rid of them.

Golden retrievers need love and attention just as much as they need food and water. Spend time with your dog every day and include it in your activities. Your golden retriever may be one of your best friends.

Quick Facts about Dogs

Dog Terms

A male is simply called a dog. A female dog is called a bitch. A young dog is a puppy until it is one year old. A newborn puppy is a whelp until it is **weaned**. A family of puppies born at one time is called a litter.

Life History

Origin:	All dogs, wolves, coyotes, and **dingoes** descended from a single wolflike dog. Dogs have been friends of humans since earliest times.
Types:	There are many colors, shapes, and sizes of dogs. Full-grown dogs weigh from two pounds (one kilogram) to more than 200 pounds (90 kilograms). They are from six inches (15 centimeters) to three feet (90 centimeters) tall. They can have thick hair or almost no hair, long or short legs, and many types of ears, faces, and tails. There are about 350 different dog breeds in the world.
Reproductive life:	Dogs mature at six to 18 months. Puppies are born two months after breeding. A female can have two litters per year. An average litter is three to six puppies, but litters of 15 or more are possible.
Development:	Puppies are born blind and deaf. Their ears and eyes open at one to two weeks. They try to walk at about two weeks. At three weeks, their teeth begin to come in, and they are ready to start weaning.

| Life span: | Dogs are fully grown at two years. If well cared for, they may live about 15 years. |

The Dog's Super Senses

Smell:	Dogs have a sense of smell many times stronger than a human's. Dogs use their supersensitive noses even more than their eyes and ears. They recognize people, animals, and objects just by smelling them, sometimes from long distances away or for days afterward.
Hearing:	Dogs hear far better than humans. Not only can dogs hear things from farther away, they can hear high-pitched sounds people cannot.
Sight:	Dogs are **color-blind**. Some scientists think dogs can tell some colors. Others think dogs see everything in black and white. Dogs can see twice as wide around them as humans can because their eyes are on the sides of their heads.
Touch:	Dogs enjoy being petted more than almost any other animal. They can feel vibrations like an approaching train or an earthquake soon to happen.
Taste:	Dogs do not taste much. This is partly because their sense of smell is so strong that it overpowers the taste. It is also partly because they swallow their food too quickly to taste it well.
Navigation:	Dogs can often find their way through crowded streets or across miles of wilderness without any guidance. This is a special dog sense that scientists do not fully understand.

Glossary

color-blind—unable to see colors or the difference between colors

dingo—wild Australian dog

distemper—a virus that is the most common disease of dogs

game—hunted wild animals and birds

guide dog—a dog trained to lead a blind person

gun dog—a dog trained to find and retrieve game that has been shot

handler—a person who trains or manages a dog for work or competition

heartworm—tiny worm carried by mosquitoes that enters a dog's heart and slowly destroys it

Lyme disease—a disease carried by ticks that causes illness, pain, and sometimes paralysis in animals and humans

muzzle—the part of a dog's head that is in front of the eyes, including the nose and mouth

pedigree—a list of an animal's ancestors

rabies—a virus spread through saliva, affecting people, pets, and wild animals, almost always deadly unless treated immediately

register—to record a dog's breeding records with a kennel club

service dog—a dog trained to help a disabled person

setter—a dog bred and trained to find and point to live game

signal dog—a dog trained to help people who cannot hear

spaniel—a small or medium-size hunting dog with long hair and drop ears

veterinarian—a person trained and qualified to treat the diseases and injuries of animals

wean—to stop nursing or depending on a mother's milk

To Learn More

Bauer, Nona Kilgore. *The World of the Golden Retriever: A Dog for All Seasons*. Neptune, N.J.: TFH Publications, 1993.

Fogle, Bruce. *Golden Retriever*. Dog Breed Handbooks. New York: DK Pub., 1996.

Huxley, Joanne P. *Guide to Owning a Golden Retriever*. Popular Dog Library. Philadelphia: Chelsea House Publishers, 1999.

McDonald, Jane. *Golden Retrievers*. Kansas City, Mo.: Andrews and McNeel, 1996.

Rosen, Michael J. *Kids' Best Dog Book*. New York: Workman, 1993.

You can read articles about golden retrievers in *AKC Gazette*, *Dog Fancy*, *Dog World*, and *Gun Dog* magazines.

Useful Addresses and Internet Sites

American Kennel Club
5580 Centerview Drive
Raleigh, NC 27606
http://www.akc.org

Canadian Kennel Club
89 Skyway Avenue
Suite 100
Etobicoke, ON M9W 6R4
Canada
http://www.ckc.ca

Dogs with Jobs
http://www.dogswithjobs.com

Golden Retriever Club of America
Edell Schafer
W 5250 S. Nicolet Dr.
New Berlin, WI 53151
http://grca.org

Golden Retriever Club of Canada
24 Carrie Street
Beaverbank, NS B4G 1B2
Canada
http://www.grcc.net

Index

ЯƎTИƎƆ CENTER

THE LEARNING RESOURCE CENTER
Weston Intermediate School